Smarter Thinking

The Uncomplicated Way to Upgrade Your Self-Image and Face Any Challenge

JOE MCNULTY

Printed in the UK

First Printing, 2020

ISBN 9781676234128

This book is dedicated to my extended family. They provide the real meaning in my life.

ABOUT THE AUTHOR

Born in Armagh, Northern Ireland, Joe McNulty worked as a secondary school English teacher for most of his career before becoming a Development Consultant with the International Fund for Ireland in 1989. Since retiring from that role in 2008 he has worked as a life coach, helping hundreds of people face all kinds of challenges. Joe has a psychology degree from Queens University, Belfast and has had a long career in Gaelic Football management. He coached the Armagh Senior team that won the Ulster title in 1983. He also managed the Mullaghbawn team during the 1980s and 1990s, and managed St. Paul's High School to an All-Ireland win in 1980. He is the father of All-Ireland winning footballers, Justin and Enda McNulty and lives with his wife Mary in Armagh. Joe, a long time SDLP activist and supporter, also describes himself as a trainee farmer and a builder of stonewalls.

PRAISE FROM JOE'S CLIENTS

"Sometimes when you are in the middle of a situation, you can't see the wood for the trees. The beauty of Joe's approach is its clarity. When the big challenges arise, it's something everyone can grasp and put into practice in everyday life."

"I followed all of Joe's ideas and listened carefully to the information he gave me about getting rid of my phobia. It all worked. My fear has been considerably alleviated, and I'm confident his approach could work for anybody."

"As a late comer to the professional world of acting I can certainly recommend Joe McNulty's approach to achieving your full potential, overcoming negativity and developing the art of the positive. He was instrumental in boosting my self confidence and getting me into the zone. Joe's approach certainly helps me both in overcoming the fear of auditioning, and in achieving the portrayal of a role. I am lucky to have him on my team."

CONTENTS

INTRODUCTION

I studied psychology in Queens University, Belfast, and was awarded a degree in that discipline in 1968, but the truth is that I never really enjoyed my course. Much of the time, I simply could not understand what the lecturers were saying. At the time, I put this down to my own inadequacies. Now, looking back, I realise that some of these teaching professionals were more interested in impressing their academic colleagues than engaging with novice students. It was, at the time, a dry, theoretical subject, taught without any reference to how life should be lived.

I went on to become an English teacher, but it wasn't until I changed career many years later that I found the version of psychology I had been looking for all my life. Writers like Martin Seligman, Bob Rotella, Maureen Gaffney and a host of others revealed a subject with all kinds of practical applications. They held out the prospect of change, of a better way of living to those, like myself, who needed it.

In the years that followed I began helping people to overcome the mental snags and hurdles that were impeding their performance. Since I had a background in sport, that's where it began but over time, I have helped people from all walks of life, suffering under all kinds of fears, phobias and difficulties.

This book is the summation of a lifetime of fascination with the workings of the human mind, and the quest to find a better way to live. It's not a lengthy work, and that's no accident. I wanted to write something short and uncomplicated, something that would help people to help themselves.

I've broken the material down into two sections. The first part introduces the ideas that are arranged into a mental workout in the second half. This workout is based on the idea of a physical workout, and like a physical workout, its power lies in commitment and repetition. You don't need a lot time on your hands to make these techniques work for you – far from it. The beauty of the system is that you can train your mind in the midst of your busy day. But you will need to commit to maintaining the workout, particularly after the novelty wears off. The rewards are well worth the effort.

Good luck!

Joe McNulty, Armagh, January 2020

Part I
Life

1
Suzanne's Story

Recently, on my 72nd birthday, a new client came to my house. Suzanne was a health professional with a pressing problem. Her husband had booked them both on a flight to Spain to celebrate a significant anniversary in a house which they owned and in which they'd shared many happy times. The problem was that she had a dreadful fear of flying. She hadn't been in her house in Spain in twelve years. Her husband thought an early booking would help to override her fear and nudge her to make a special effort. I had helped the son of a colleague of this woman, a young man whose poor self confidence and low self esteem were affecting his academic performance. But could I help with this issue?

The first thing Suzanne asked me was whether or not she should cancel her flight, which was due to take off in almost exactly three weeks, on May 16th. Her last flight, twelve years earlier, had been a nightmare. The way she put it was that her body had been in riot; palpitations, sweating, a terrible sense of foreboding. The flight attendants had helped her to get through it, but when the plane touched down, she swore that that was it. Never again. In the intervening time, her fear had become so acute that even the thought of flying was enough to trigger a panic attack. So now she had arrived at decision time. Would she cancel or could I help her?

This Stuff Works

I told Suzanne what I tell everyone who comes to me with problems, which is that I have no magic solution. I have however been a student of psychology for most of my life, and have distilled all of my experience and reading on the subject into a short course. I usually deliver this one-on-one, sometimes to small groups, in four or five one-hour sessions, each a week apart.

In short, this course shows the client how to adopt new enabling habits and leave behind habits which hold them back. The first thing I do with a new client is encourage them to shed one small unwanted habit and use my system to put a helpful habit in its place. For example, one might attempt to discontinue the habit of losing one's cool in traffic and replace it with the habit of keeping calm. This may sound insignificant, and perhaps it is, but success with something small can be very helpful in asserting the value of the approach. It can demonstrate that *this stuff works*.

I don't suggest that this course is either comprehensive or failsafe. What it does however – and what I hope this book will do too – is provide a means of exercising greater control over our thought processes. Over the last fifteen years, I have helped scores of clients to achieve their goals, to overcome obstacles and to lead fuller, happier lives.

I may be able to impart the theory and practice but the outcome is wholly dependent on the efforts of each client. The good news is that the workouts I draft for each one do not take up huge chunks of time. They consist of three easily remembered parts, two dealing with negative self-talk and one with future challenges. I'm going to go into more detail about these in the second half of this little book. First, I want to continue with Suzanne's story.

I had to explain to her that I could not guarantee success, and now, with a deadline twenty days away...Well, we agreed to give it a go. In normal circumstances, I would recommend continuing the workouts for five weeks before tackling a serious challenge. Given the tight timeline, I decided to intensify the process a little. Suzanne came in for three two-hour sessions that weekend. During those sessions, I coached her on the workout she would need to do repeatedly over the coming weeks in order to reset her emotional and physical reactions to taking a flight.

Virtual Travel

What did this involve? I required Suzanne to create, in her mind, a simulation of the challenge ahead. I explained to her that she needed to travel virtually from Belfast International to Malaga Airport at least eight times a day over the next sixteen days. Imagining the entire flight was unnecessary; each rehearsal would take between one and two minutes. Nor did she have to sit silently in a darkened room to facilitate these simulations. Suzanne had trouble believing me when I told her that these workouts would take no time out of her day. These are *thinking* exercises, and can be done at the same time as so many daily chores. In the days that followed, Suzanne performed several reps in the shower, while doing her hair and clearing the dishwasher. Her daily walk gave her the opportunity to complete several more reps, as did numerous other tasks, all of which were sufficiently routine to leave the mind free to do as it pleased. This is one of the most pleasing elements of the process; it fits so well with the busy lives that we all lead. You do not need to set aside time to bring about significant change, you only need the discipline to continue the workouts through the designated timeframe.

As for the workouts themselves, these visualisations were enacted using only the tools which Suzanne already possessed – her five senses, her emotions and her imagination; her ability to generate action and atmosphere. I helped her to imagine boarding the plane, to feel the gangway beneath her feet, to hear the chatter of people finding their seats and the beeps and grinding noises of a plane getting ready to fly. I coached her to feel the headrest under her hand as she found her seat, to feel herself being pushed deeper into the seat as the plane accelerated down the runway. I coached her to do all this but without feelings of anxiety and panic. These would be replaced with a sense of contentment and control.

Our agreed target was that she would complete in excess of 120 repeats of the rehearsal in the days ahead. I suggested that she keep May 15th – the day before the flight – free to relax and prepare for the holiday.

Later, Suzanne told me that she had meticulously repeated the rehearsal 16 times a day – twice the number I had advised. That made it more than 250 times she had, in her mind, boarded the plane, sat in her seat, taken off and landed before she ever set foot in the airport.

On May16th, I was out having dinner with my wife and a few friends when my phone buzzed. It was a text from Suzanne. She had just landed in Malaga Airport.

Who-hoo Joe! We did it! Calm relaxed but giddy!

She told me afterwards that she was so enraptured with the transformation that she felt like a child on Christmas morning. In advance of the return flight, she did what she termed a 'toned down' version of these mental rehearsals and everything went fine.

The final point I want to make in this chapter is that Suzanne's giddy text from Malaga Airport wasn't entirely accurate. 'We did it', she wrote. In reality, *we* did nothing. She was the author of her own achievement. When we first spoke, she talked of panic attacks so severe she could not imagine herself getting on a plane ever again. It was simply too frightening. Twenty days later she got on a plane and experienced a relatively comfortable flight. She alone had found the motivation to share her dilemma with a work colleague. She had desperately wanted to accompany her husband to the house where they had spent so many good times together. She went looking for a solution, and when she found one that might work, she was brave enough to give it a go.

2
The Plane that nearly Crashed

I was able to help Suzanne for a variety of reasons, not least the fact that I grew up with a fear of flying. For whatever reason, I had always been what I came to call a white-knuckle flier; always anxious, always fearful, reacting to every pulse and shudder of the aircraft, every thrust of the engines. Despite all this, I took flights regularly, and even commuted to Toronto for two years. All this changed after an emergency landing in Dublin Airport in the late eighties. The curious thing about it is that it wasn't even my experience, it was my wife's.

The Flight
I had driven Mary to the airport to catch a flight to London. A party from the school where we both then taught was travelling to do some Christmas shopping and to see Arsenal play Spurs. Big Pat Jennings was in goal for Spurs at the time, and his brother Brian was a colleague of ours at the school. Co-incidentally, their sister Marie, who was a flight attendant, was also present, as was the late broadcaster, Gay Byrne.

Seconds after take-off, the port engine suffered a critical loss of power, causing the wing to dip alarmingly close to the runway. The pilot immediately called all flight staff into the cockpit and instructed passengers to adopt emergency protocols. The plan was to dump fuel at sea and return to attempt an emergency landing. This he did safely after twenty minutes of extreme anxiety for the adults and an exciting adventure for the youngsters.

Because I knew so many of those on board, I heard many detailed accounts of those harrowing minutes. I heard of the pilot's extreme concern, the terror of the passengers and the anxiety on the faces of the flight attendants as they exited the flight deck. And of course I was an English teacher with a first year class who were skilled in coaxing me – 'Aw Sir, tell us that story again about the plane that nearly crashed...'

So I told the story over and over, emphasising the terrified behaviour of some of the teachers, and the amusement of the children who did not appreciate the danger. With each re-telling, the story became more and more dramatic, the details more intense.

Even though I had not been present on the flight, even though I had not experienced the anxiety, my second-hand experience became so powerful that the manageable fear of flying I had known up to this point now became unmanageable. The near-death experience, augmented by my dramatised re-telling, fed that fear. It got to a point where if I saw a low-flying jet as I walked near my home, I would experience a frightening physical spasm in my chest – in effect, the beginnings of a panic attack.

Unwittingly, I had been doing the opposite of what I now coach my clients to do. I had been enacting emotionally charged visualisations of a near-death experience. And so that was it. I could no longer fly.

Investment in Excellence

Cut to ten years later. By then, I had changed career and was working with a community group in Newry on an economic regeneration project set up during the Northern Ireland peace process. A recommendation from a colleague prompted me to sign up for a course called *Investment in Excellence.* I thought that this course related to economic appraisal, which was an important element of the work we had been doing. I was wrong. As soon as the facilitator started speaking that morning, I knew that this was the course I had been looking for all my life. That *Investment in Excellence* course, run over three days in 1993, was the catalyst that sparked an all-consuming interest. Over the 25 years that elapsed since then, I have become a dedicated student of cognitive psychology.

There are two formative experiences in my personal history that provided a fertile ground for this fascination.

My Mother

My mother returned to Northern Ireland from Philadelphia in 1932 and took on a role as a hard-working farmer's wife on a small holding in South Armagh. She continued happily in this role until 1973 when changes on the farm left her largely redundant. The loss of this role, and the failure to find one to replace it, led to a deep depression which

13

from which she never recovered, and in 1976, she took her own life. I have to say that even in the immediate aftermath of this tragedy, I admired her courage in taking the only action which she believed could release her from the suffering I had seen on her face. But I wanted to understand more about why my mother, who had a long and happy life, would take such a step after three years of depression. My reading over the last twenty five years has taught me that I will not find the answer, but I am more content now that I have a better understanding of what she went through.

The second experience is sport-related. When I began work as an English teacher at a boy's secondary school, my playing experience as a Gaelic footballer led to my appointment as coach of the senior team. In that role, I learned a great deal about my lack of expertise in preparing a team for the varying demands of competition.

Getting Your Hands on the Steering Wheel
Lou Tice, the man who devised the *Investment in Excellence* course that had such a profound influence on me, had also been an English teacher and a football coach, and he too had been unhappy with how these subjects were respectively taught and coached. He too had gone to university to study psychology, but his university experience was very different to mine. His lecturers did not present him with a dry, theoretical subject, utterly removed from everyday life. They showed him how psychology could be a practical subject that could help you to

make better choices. His teachers, and the course he would go on to devise, suggested that we normal human beings could – indeed should – play an active role in the running of our lives. Rather than accept out experiences as inevitable and subject to the whimsical spin of circumstance, we can get our hands on the steering wheel of our own lives. I learned that we don't always control what happens, but we can learn to control how we react both to what has happened and to what is likely to happen in the future.

In the aftermath of that course, my reading took off. From Lou Tice, I went to Tim Gallwey and Bob Rotella. I discovered cognitive psychology and read Martin Seligman and Maureen Gaffney, together with a host of other great practical psychologists. I had been wandering in a wilderness of doubt and anxiety for years, but now I realised that there was something I could do about the problems that beset my own life. I had a choice. My self-image was not set in stone. Second nature was not an inherited immoveable certainty; it was called 'second' for a reason.

All of these liberating discoveries launched me into action and have kept me active ever since.

To those who accuse me of succumbing to the self-help bug, my answer is simple. What would you do if you found an authentic method of shedding baggage accumulated through life, all the things that were slowing you down and hampering your growth?

And anyhow, what's so bad about wanting to help yourself?

And I suppose, most of the disdain aimed at the self-help movement has been earned by those offering less than scientific advice, often suggesting mysterious, and sometimes magical sources for their powers. Many of these make strenuous attempts to discredit anything other than their version of the truth. I do none of that.

I have tried to read only authentic academic psychologists and proven coaches. And I let my life experience speak for me.

Learning to Fly

My most practical personal lesson occurred when the designated tutor from The Pacific Institute, which ran the *Investment in Excellence* course, became ill just before a group session I had arranged in Belfast. When I rang London for an alternative, the director of the institute, David Tate, said, "That's no problem Joe. You were a teacher, you've attended the course three times. You do it. Come over to London next week for two days and we'll train you up."

"That's going to be a bit of a problem, David. I don't fly."

David's reaction left me with little choice. "You're arranging this course for others but you haven't learnt the first principle. Start with yourself."

To cut a long story short, I got to work and flew to London ten days later having prepared for a flight which was relatively free of fear.

Over the last ten years, I've coached students taking exams, candidates facing job interviews, kids lacking self-belief, together with a wide variety of sports people – golfers, soccer players, rugby players and hurlers. I've coached young people suffering from clinical depression and helped clients overcome a wide variety of phobias.

A central message of this is that high self esteem and self-confidence are not traits that you are born with. They are not accidents of birth, they are not reserved for the privileged few, but can be learned and developed.

The rest of this book condenses all I have learned over the years. I hope that it is written in a style which my son describes as 'Sesame Street simple'.

Get Out Clause

With each new client, I insist on an initial half-hour meeting where I explain my approach. Attempting to coach against the grain would be an entirely fruitless experience for both of us, so if the client is deeply sceptical or does not believe in the capacity of the ordinary human being to grow and change, we do not proceed. In all the years I have been teaching this course, only one person has ever opted out.

3
The Perception Problem

My first task is to demonstrate to the client that his or her perception of reality is just that – a perception, that there are other ways of looking at the same thing.

A man came to me a little while back with problems on the golf course. He always lost his temper when luck seemed to turn against him. Like many clients, he maintained that this character trait was fixed and unchangeable.

"That's just the way I am! I know myself well enough to know that."

I explained to him that far from being a set in stone, this characteristic was no more than a bad habit developed in the face of challenging experiences. I then pointed out to him that all humans are subject to similar patterns of behaviour.

When I was younger, I was convinced that I had a firm handle on reality. I knew my strengths and weaknesses. I believed that I would never have much confidence because I didn't have much to be confident about. The reason Suzanne could not fly is because she saw herself as a person who would never be able to calmly board an aircraft. Was this perception real? Was my own image of myself as a younger man real?

Take a look at this sentence:

FINISHED FILES ARE THE RESULT OF MANY YEARS OF SCIENTIFIC STUDY COMBINED WITH THE EXPERIENCE OF MANY YEARS.

I'm now going to carry out a brief experiment. It is not a test of your intelligence or your ability to comprehend. But I want you to re-read the sentence carefully for meaning only. Now, read it again, but this time concentrate on finding any letter Fs in the sentence. Can I encourage you to think only of the letter F, and the distinct F sound. Don't take any more than a few seconds

Now act! Count, as quickly as you can, the letter Fs. Write the number you find on a note pad.

Now a different focus. Count the number of the words spelled 'of' in the sentence. How many did you get? Is the number of Fs you recorded earlier still correct?

If there is a difference, can you explain how you failed to see all the Fs in your first reading ? In my course I use four or five similar illustrations to draw attention to common human misperceptions.

My intention in using these illustrations is to demonstrate a fundamental tendency in human beings. We sometimes fail to see what is in front of our eyes. We have blind-spots.

In his book, *Thinking Fast and Slow*, Nobel Laureate Daniel Kahneman explains that humans are subject to tendencies and biases which blind us to information which should be obvious.

He has demonstrated that we're not as rational as we like to think we are, and that inbuilt biases, assumptions and tendencies frequently send us in the wrong direction. He talks for example about overconfidence bias, which is often to blame for mistakes in decision making. Susceptibility to these blind-spots has very little to do with our intelligence. It's almost as if our perception has been pre-programmed in some way; and not only our sight, but our hearing, our sense of touch, smell, taste and even our emotions cooperate to shut out incoming information which should be obvious.

Another telling example of this is Kahneman's famous selective attention test, which I've sometimes used in my courses. To offer one example, I was asked by the principal of a grammar school to give a talk to senior staff – some eighty teachers – on the relevance of sports psychology to teaching. I started by showing them a video, where a group of people pass a basketball between them while moving about a court. Before hitting the 'play' button, I asked the teachers to count the number of passes thrown by the team dressed in white. I mentioned, as an aside, that females had been found to do better on this test than males. This I had made up, just to confuse the issue a little. Halfway through the video, someone dressed in a gorilla suit enters the frame, walks through the middle of the players and out the other side. Afterwards, when I asked who had seen the gorilla, only about half raised their hands. The rest looked at me as if I was mad. Gorilla? What gorilla? It was very amusing to see the looks on their faces when I replayed the video and all now saw what should have been blindingly obvious the first time around. The conclusion is that when our attention is focused on one thing, we tend to fail to see other details, no matter how obvious they appear in hindsight.

Does this mean that there is something wrong with us? On the contrary. According to Kahneman, it simply shows that we humans have a tendency to sometimes fail to see what is in front of our eyes. And we fail to hear, sense, smell or taste, things which should have been obvious.

Nowhere is this failure more entrenched than in the human self-image.

Self Image
Self image is every bit as real as the physical image you see in the mirror in the morning. We constantly ask ourselves, what sort of parent am I? What sort of wife? What am I like in a crisis? Am I good at my job? These questions and hundreds like them swim through our minds constantly, sometimes consciously, sometimes unconsciously. The answers coalesce to form our self-image, and as we have seen, there is a great tendency among humans to think this image fixed. We know our own reality, do we not?

In my coaching of individuals and groups in sports or life issues, I cannot recall meeting one individual who had a clear, authentic view of his or her own ability. The great majority held opinions slanted *against* themselves. They underestimated their potential. Few gave themselves credit for their strengths; most emphasised their weaknesses. A skewed perception about your own reality seems to be endemic to humanity.

More critically, few I have met have appreciated the influence this had on the quality of their performance. The obvious point to make is that if they came to me for advice, then each had some perceived problem, but I am confident most people who never ask for professional advice feel the same way. And many are not aware how this self-image acts as a limiter on performance in everything we do. It's like a built in regulator, constantly updated by our own thinking, whether consciously or not. The eminent golf coach, Dr Bob Rotella puts it this way:

"I see evidence of the influence of the subconscious self-image in all the golfers I counsel. In many of them, the subconscious influences their scores as predictably as a thermostat regulates the temperature in a house."

I believe that this condition applies across all sport, and indeed across performance in life in general. You dwell on the bad rather than the good, and fool yourself into thinking that this is simply being mature, being realistic. But because of this bias, you limit your own performance and so become the bad performer you believe yourself to be. It's the classic self-fulfilling prophecy.

It may be a surprise to learn that most of your daily functioning falls under the control of the unconscious mind rather than the conscious mind, Your temperature, your cardiovascular functioning, your digestive systems...these motor functions operate at an unseen level beyond the jurisdiction of the conscious mind. Likewise, all of our deep-seated habits and attitudes function outside the influence of the conscious mind. Fervent and sincere action will not bring about lasting change, certainly not on its own.

In her book, *Flourishing,* Professor Maureen Gaffney says, 'We use that free will not nearly as much as we would like to believe. In fact a large part of our everyday life is determined by powerful automatic mental processes that operate outside our awareness. This is largely why our many well-intentioned efforts to achieve our goals and change ourselves can fail.'

The Simulator
Thus, the traditional model of teaching and learning based on good honest effort, hard work and determination loses out to a more effective method, influenced by our subconscious self-image. This more powerful model involves our ability to communicate directly with our own subconscious mind. Do this effectively and you can get rid of habits that hold you back and replace them with habits that make living richer. No one else can do this but ourselves alone, and relatively few of us know how.

There is however a group of professionals privileged to experience training which is focused on the sub-conscious mind. I'm talking about airline pilots. No matter how good a trainee pilot's intellect and aptitude, they are not allowed near the controls of a commercial aircraft until they have been trained in a simulator. This is a sophisticated machine which simulates – to a very high degree of accuracy – the actual functioning of the aircraft. The aim of this training is to make the pilot's reactions as automatic as possible. The aim is to allow the pilot to bypass the conscious mind and respond before the conscious mind even perceives the problem.

Why should these already exceptional candidates be trained in simulators? What is it about the simulator that makes it so crucial in training pilots? My answer is that the simulator is not about tutoring the intellect. Rather, it is focused on the subconscious mind, that part of our brain which controls our automatic performance. It enhances the pilot's spontaneous mastery of skills and dexterity, way beyond anything achievable by conventional training.

I also want to touch on the use of subconscious training in the sporting world. In their role alongside coaches and managers, professional sport psychologists concentrate on those automatic, spontaneous, free flowing skills which lie beyond the immediate influence of our conscious awareness. Athletes don't use sophisticated machines to train their minds, they use something far more advanced – the mind itself. They harness the imagination to communicate with the subconscious mind.

Why should athletes, because they are thought to have talent, be privileged to enjoy this sort of training while the rest of us must be content with conventional methods? The aim of this book is to allow anyone to learn techniques similar to those used routinely by pilots and athletes, and which in turn can be as easily applied to everyday life as to a cockpit or a sports arena.

Change is Possible

We have seen a lot of research over the last decade which has revealed much about the facility of humans to continue to develop their mental capacities throughout their lives.

Michael Merzenich is an American neuroscientist who's done pioneering work in the area of brain plasticity. His research has proven that the brain isn't hardwired at all, but can actually re-wire itself continually over the course of your life. He believes that 'brain aerobics' should form part of a well organised life, in just the same way that physical exercise does.

This is what he says:

'Science is telling us that you are in charge, that it's under your control, that your happiness, your well-being, your abilities, your capacities, are capable of continuous modification, continuous improvement, and you're the responsible agent and party.'

Similarly, neuroscientist, Richard Restak, in his book *Think Smart*, suggests that a well-planned mental workout is very important for well-being and brain function. His basic thesis is that cognitive functioning is modifiable.

"..Mental acuity, knowledge and information, memory, speed of information processing, curiosity, and the ability to think in abstract terms and related to specific applications, can be improved by one's own efforts."

Knowing exactly which areas of your life need attention is of course central to enacting a strategy to begin to adapt your thinking. Chances are you've been drawn to this book and have gotten this far because you know precisely where the problem lies. This would also be true of most of my clients.

In the last two years, I've helped people with problems losing their temper, their focus, their energy and enthusiasm. I've dealt with athletes who could perform well in practice but not in competition. If you have any doubt about where the problem lies, an online diagnostic tool like 'The Wheel of Life' is very helpful. This takes a holistic look at the entirety of your life and can help to identify aspects causing most concern.

Once you know which area of life you wish to improve, or which obstacle you want to overcome, the next step is to begin working out.

Part II
The Workout

4
Self-talk

Up to this point, I've talked about the experiences which have prompted me to write this book in the first place and explained something about how I help people. I now want to discuss the workout in detail.

If you're physically out of shape, an exercise routine will be central to getting you back to your best. It's just the same with your mental wellbeing. The right workout can help you to dispense with behaviours and attitudes that are no longer serving you, and help to adopt new ones which will. If you want to flourish, you will need to adopt the right lifestyle habits.

For any mental workout to be effective, it must comply with three basic criteria.

- It must be short enough so that it will be easy to remember and repeat
- It must be sufficiently simple that the concepts underlying it can be explained in one sitting.
- Taken together, the components of the workout must form a bundle of activity which transforms mental functioning.

Here then are the three elements of the workout:

1. Ending negative self-talk
2. Imprinting helpful self-talk
3. Using visualisation to meet life's challenges

We'll take each in turn.

Ending Negative Self-talk

Most of us have a tendency to generate thoughts and self-talk which are critical of self. In the days following a painful episode, when you were shamed or upset by something you did, these thoughts will recur over and over again. Invariably, as I have discussed, we tend to accept these perceptions as fact. You will tell yourself, *That's just the way I am.* The truth however is that you have far more choice in the matter than you think.

To change anything, the first step is awareness. Scientists estimate that on average we humans sustain about 50,000 thoughts each day, of which we are consciously aware of about 20%. So much of this self-talk is so subtle and so constant that we just don't notice it.

It's time to notice it.

Documenting Negative Self-Talk

ACTION: Start a journal, on a device or in a notebook that you keep with you. In this journal, record and date your most dominant thoughts in relation to the various challenges you meet. Do this religiously for two weeks, recording five or more instances of negative self-talk every day. How do you rate yourself on your performance at work? Your interactions with others? Your performance at sport?

Here are three examples of the sort of thing I'm talking about:

- July 3rd: I made a mess of that speech at the meeting. People laughed at me rather than my jokes. I'm no good at speaking.
- July 5th: I was ashamed when the manager told me that I didn't get the promotion. I'm clearly incompetent at my job.
- I must have looked a right fool when I missed that simple tap-in goal yesterday. It's time I gave up football. I'm just no good under pressure.
- July 27th: When I went to exercise class the new teacher told me I was too old for that sort of thing. I had to go home. Recalled that a lot last night. Woke up this morning with the thought on my mind.

Not all of our thoughts are self-critical but it is the nature of humankind to focus relentlessly on things that go wrong in one way or another. In subsequent days, you remember these painful events. You replay the video in your mind and suffer the shame and embarrassment over and over again. With each repetition, the conviction that you are a failure sinks deeper and deeper into your psyche.

ACTION: The next step is to take each of these opinions – for that is what they are, not facts – and submit them to the truth test. Remember, each of these critical thoughts is more than just the firing of neurons within the brain. They are powerful performance inhibitors. If you believe yourself no good at something, it follows as night follows day that you will be no good at it. Challenge the validity of the self critical thought. Examine each objectively and forensically.

- *I'm no good at speaking.* Is this really true? Yes, I stumbled in a speech at work yesterday, yes, I felt intense embarrassment as a result. But does this mean that I'm no good at public speaking? I wasn't that well prepared for the speech – I'd been busy all week with other priorities and thought I could wing it. I hadn't rehearsed. Perhaps I could do better if I rehearsed. In fact, I'm sure I could do better if I prepared better. It stands to reason.
- *I'm incompetent at my job.* Is this really true? Yes, I did not perform well in the interview, and I'm not as experienced as the person who got the job. Recently, I haven't been performing well, my mind hasn't been on my job. Certainly, if I think back, there have been many occasions where I have done well. Perhaps if I improved my focus and energy levels, I could rekindle my enthusiasm for my job and do better.
- *It's time I gave up football. I'm no good under pressure.* Is this really true? What actually happened? Just as I was kicking for goal, my other foot slipped, and I hadn't had much kicking practise recently because I was recovering from a sprained ankle. Maybe I do need to do a little more practice, and maybe I

32

do need to work on my mental toughness, but I have been good under pressure before, and can be again.

- *I'm too old for exercise.* Being sent home because I'm too old was a horrible experience but is it really true? Am I really too old? Perhaps the new teacher was afraid I would get into difficulty if I tried those exercises; he was young and probably a little inexperienced. He perhaps didn't feel confident enough to take someone of my age through the class. He didn't know that I've been attending other exercise classes and have been doing just fine. Perhaps I should speak to the manager about the issue, or talk to my doctor about exactly what level of exercise I can safely tolerate. And even if there's one form of exercise I shouldn't do anymore, there are plenty of alternatives.

The habit of rehearsing the negative belief can often happen below the level of full awareness, and yet it can have a profound effect on our capabilities. It can take serious effort to bring an end to this cycle of negative thought and poor performance. Take the time to journal each of these negative thoughts and submit them to the full glare of your rational mind. Is your negative self-image real?

I always ask my clients this question: 'Do you love yourself?' I'm not trying to be funny. Love of self is vital in creating a fertile habitat for the growth of confidence.

By forensically submitting each of these negative thoughts to the truth test, you can begin to see just how false your negative view of yourself is. This is the first step to removing the self-defeating habit of critical self-talk and replacing it with a perception of yourself that is both truthful and positive. This will allow you to get into the habit of figuring out what you can learn from these mistakes and transform your self-talk into something that helps rather than holds you back.

While all of this may be seen as an interesting, for it to become more than that, for it to have a significant impact on your life, you must commit to scheduling time to document and examine your self-talk as described above. You need to allow time to do this work at least three times a week in order to generate lasting change.

I think of one 19 year old client who awarded himself a four out of ten as a measure of his respect and love of self. I explained how difficult it was for anyone with such a low opinion of himself to learn and grow. He quickly accepted that his first priority was to revise this opinion. When all the deceptive negative stuff was filtered out, what remained was a self-image he could trust.

5
Imprinting helpful self-talk

I now want to look at self-talk from another angle. This perspective draws on work done by eminent psychologist Martin Seligman, regarded as the father of positive psychology. Both he – in his book *Flourish* – and psychologist Maureen Gaffney in her book *Flourishing* point out that negative self-talk is four times more powerful than positive self-talk. Most of us share this inbuilt tendency to accentuate the negative, to give bad news more weight than good news. To counter this impulse, Seligman devised a simple exercise – What Went Well, or WWW for short. This has proved so successful in improving self-image that it has been embraced, along with many other positive psychology techniques, by the US army.

What Went Well
This exercise is all about keeping a daily record of things that go well in some way. It can relate to any facet of life, but pay particular attention to episodes in which you played a direct role, no matter how small. It could be anything from a chance meeting with an old friend to something as slight as holding the door open for someone. Did you do well at work? Did you create something new? Were you kind to someone? Daily practice at recalling and recording what went well for a period of 21 days has been shown to have a very significant positive impact on self image.

I suggest that recording your recollection is not enough. Just as it remains a human habit to repeatedly replay the negative incident, you are now free to recall and dwell upon the good stuff. Go ahead and relive it all, using all of the sensory tools at your disposal. And, as before, this process doesn't need to take up any time. You just develop the habit of replaying – in every glorious detail – all of the things that have gone well in the recent past. Make it part of your day-to-day routine.

ACTION: Open a new notebook, or start a new document on your device. At the end of each day, record three items that went well over the course of the day. Alongside each, say *why* they went well. As you go to sleep, recall each of these items and replay the event repeatedly, so that you relive the pleasurable experience again and again before you drop off.

As with the practices detailed in the last chapter, in order for this process to have lasting impact, you must commit to daily repetition. Replaying these positive experiences will only become second nature in this way.

As one who has put this into action, I can say it has worked for me. My habit of wakening to a mental flip-chart of recent failures and shameful cock-ups has been replaced by a new tendency to recall the highlights of the last few days. And no longer do I squirm at mistakes or failures, nor do I try to mentally dismiss them. Now I simply ask myself, what can I learn from this? How will I approach this scenario in future?

The new habit has a side-effect. A lighter mood. I smile more. I laugh at myself every day. There's nothing better than that to enhance your mood. And any time I look back over my journal I am pleased to read about how most things turned out well.

I find too that I have become less afraid of making mistakes. Obviously you don't set out in a game or an assignment to make a mistake, but with this attitude, you are willing to take risks. Then, if the mistake does happen, you welcome it as a learning aid, not as something to be hushed up and shamed by. You learn from each mistake and become a more competent worker/performer.

6
Using visualisation to meet life's challenges

Professional sports coaches and performers call it visualisation. Actors call it rehearsal. They *pre*-enact performance, combine it with deliberate physical practice and the authenticity of the imagined act contributes to the quality of the actual performance. These techniques may be used regularly by professional actors and elite athletes, but you do not have to have extraordinary talent in order to employ them. We're talking once more about your built-in simulator, your imagination.

This is our personal version of the flight simulator, used in the training of pilots so that they are prepared for any eventuality that may challenge the safety of the aircraft they are flying. The key thing to realise is that it's not just the ability to fly the aircraft that is enhanced by the simulator, but the *intuitive response* of each pilot, which is quicker than the speed of thought. In other words the practice of visualisation can give you the ability to perform skills in sport or life in a similar fashion. Some call it 'Flow'. Your response becomes second nature, allowing you to become sufficiently bullet proof to withstand the pressures that come our way.

I sometimes find that when I introduce clients to this approach, they worry that their pre-enactment of an upcoming challenge will be faulty or incomplete. After all, few of us in our adult lives are asked to engage our imaginations with such freedom. Playing pretend is a habit most of us lost years ago, but this should not discourage you. A little practise will re-engage a facility that you never really lose.

In Suzanne's case, the challenge she faced was taking a flight. With other clients I have seen over the years, it has been a job interview, a series of exams, a sporting event and any number of experiences that promised stress.

Walking the Walk
I'd like to show you how I go about kick-starting this process with clients, how I help them to rediscover their imaginative facility and use it to create effective visualisations.

I take the client outside and ask them to accompany me in silence on a two minute walk. During this walk, we pass several different species of tree, cross a stile in a stone wall, pass through a gateway marked by two stone pillars and finally ascend three stone steps. Once complete, I ask how much of the experience they recalled. Most report very little. After all, it was very short, and in any case, I never instructed them to retain anything.

Now, I ask the client to repeat the walk – alone – but this time to engage all of their senses. See the trees, the pillars and so on, feel the breeze, hear the birdsong and the sound of their own footsteps. Above all, I ask them to register their emotions throughout their walk.

Once they do this, they report a much richer experience.

Finally, I ask them to repeat the walk in their imagination. Armed now with all of that emotional and sensory data, they are capable of re-creating the walk in their mind in great detail.

Each client now has a simple template which they can use to relive any experience. More importantly, they can use the same technique to pre-live an upcoming episode, whatever it might be. Just like Suzanne before getting on the flight, they can create a mental rehearsal of the upcoming challenge by using the sensory detail of an earlier episode. Then, by repeating this imaginative experience overlaid with positive emotion, a new attitude takes root in the subconscious, and an old, negative experience is overwritten with positive emotions. With each repeat, the self-image takes note of a growing level of confidence.

In the worlds of Lou Tice, 'Our minds are far more powerful than anyone can imagine.'

As I write this, I can feel the buzz of excitement in my stomach, the same tingle I experienced in my own efforts to challenge both my fear of flying and my tendency to worry too much.

Snow White, Walk Disney's first feature length animation was so successful and ground-breaking because he instructed his animators to replicate every nuance of an expression, to make his characters as lifelike as possible. I have found that the subconscious mind has the ingenious capacity to fill in the gaps in any pre-lived episode. So don't fret about how well you create an event in your mind. The genius of that mysterious, instinctive skill is to fill in all the missing brush strokes to help to modify our future habits.

You are in Control of You

These pre-lives put you in the driving seat. You no longer look towards a challenging event with fear and anxiety. You experience excitement instead of debilitating doubt and uncertainty. It is a curious transformation which finds you welcoming the fear as an ally in achieving your goal. For many I have coached, this can be a bit daunting when they hear it first. But once they learn that this fear, this nervousness is something that precedes an event that is increasingly under their control, I see them grow in confidence.

I have frequently observed too that this growth in confidence can often come very early in the process. It appears that turning to face the challenge head on; engaging the mind in tackling the problem is a very empowering thing to do.

Many of those that I have coached were convinced that circumstances or fate played the lead role in their lives. My job was to show them that this couldn't be further from the truth. Yes there are chance events that have a massive effect on our lives but in general each individual should assume a central role in determining what they do and how they do it. So rather than accepting fate, we need to become confident in planning our future, accepting there may be good and bad times ahead but willing to take responsibility for our own actions and ultimately for our ongoing lives. We can't always control or influence what will happen but most often we have the ability to habituate how we react to what has happened. This is a key outcome of this workout. We seize control of our own lives.

I coached a professional actor recently who kept failing in auditions because his confidence levels were so low. He could not remember his lines and always needed the script in his hand. This interfered hugely with his performance. Within weeks of trying these techniques, his acting coach remarked on a transformation in his confidence, and he began to secure parts with much greater frequency.

On another occasion, a father came to me with a peculiar problem. His three sons played sport at a high level, but every time he went to watch them play, he would be become so nervous and agitated that he would almost lose control of himself on the sideline. No one in his wider family would accompany him to games. He could not stay in one place during a match but had to move up and down the line, experiencing such feelings of tension that his doctor advised him to stop going for the good of his health. This, he could not do. Over four sessions spread over six weeks, he was able to take much better control of his emotional reactions and went on to enjoy his sons' matches for good ten years after that.

I too have found that these techniques have revolutionised my own confidence and enthusiasm levels. My energy lasts hours at a time, I feel the buzz of anticipation rather than the crippling weight of doubt. When I take on a new challenge like a flight or a speech, when I am giving a new course, I am full of enthusiasm and excitement. At my age!

I have also witnessed an unexpected side effect of my regular workouts. It's hard to accept some setbacks; losing a good friend, getting sacked, relationship problems, major failures. The side effect I experienced was, and is, that a trauma no longer inflicts as painful an impact as before I began my workouts. I am stronger, more able to withstand the incoming psychological missiles which used to penetrate my inner wellbeing. Now, I don't wish difficulties on myself, but I know I am better prepared to take what comes.

Trigger sentence
ACTION: Take a specific upcoming challenge: Attending an interview, making a speech, writing a book, playing a match, beginning a new job or a new course. Now, ask yourself: How will I perform if I am at my best?

In answering this question, you need to do two things:

1. Engage the emotions. State how you will feel if you can up your performance to the point where you are reaching your potential.
2. Root that statement in the here and now.

This will allow you to frame what I call the trigger sentence. Here are some examples:

- *I am thrilled that I now deliver my speech in an interesting and competent way.*
- *I am delighted to be fully engaged with my job and performing to the best of my ability.*
- *I am very happy to be taking a full part in my exercise class and getting all of the physical activity I need.*
- *I am thrilled to be playing to the best of my ability, with great confidence and enthusiasm.*
- *I am delighted that I am able to take a flight without any anxiety.*

You get the idea. Your trigger sentence is written as a personal goal or action plan, is always in the present tense and always revolves around positive emotion. The trigger sentence then becomes the launch-pad of your work-out. As children, we were all expert in playing pretend. To ignite the work-out, you'll need to rekindle the childhood facility for imagining. Just as the flight simulator communicates with the subconscious mind of the pilot, you use your own inbuilt simulator – your imagination – to communicate with your own subconscious. Engage all five senses and your range of emotions to bring the ideas to life in your mind. Just as Suzanne used this natural human facility to overcome her phobia, you can use the same method to rehearse a new positive scenario and over-write the negative shame-filled or mistake-ridden one.

Our faltering speaker can in this way transform his opinion of his potential within twenty-one days. The workout will begin with the aforementioned trigger sentence - *I am thrilled that I now deliver my speech in an interesting and competent way.* Next comes one to two minutes of imaginative sensory visualisation, where you mentally recreate – as precisely as possible – the circumstances of the speech. You see the expectant faces before you, feel the wooden table top beneath your arms, hear the sound of your voice – strong and confident – as you deliver your speech.

The applications of this approach are many and various. A young footballer came to me recently in order to help him address his uncontrollable temper. If the referee made a call with which he disagreed, he would fly off the handle, and often land himself in deeper trouble. His driving too was affected by his temper. The slightest provocation on the road would prompt a response that was both aggressive and dangerous.

After those early sessions he understood that he was giving up control of himself on the pitch and on the road, but after about a month of visualisations he succeeded in taking back control, of learning new habits which allowed him to stay cool intuitively, despite the provocations.

That idea – that we have far more control over our actions than we think – was pivotal in helping another young client to change his behaviour. He came to me disillusioned and demotivated having lost interest in his college course. I pointed out to him that we were not stooges in the face of circumstance. The idea that you either have it or you don't is a misleading belief from a less enlightened era. We all can learn and grow to the limit of our potential but we must first exercise the wonderful gift of choice. A year after our meetings, this young man secured a first in a college in the UK.

The formula
1 to 2 minutes X 8 times per day for 20 days = 320 minutes of imaginative visualisation = new habit.

The wonderful thing about this approach is how little time it takes up. Moreover, you can complete these short workouts while the body is physically engaged in something else. Out for a walk, sitting in a waiting room, brushing your teeth, standing in the shower...there will be so many opportunities in your everyday routine. This is exactly what Suzanne did to transform from a panic-attack prone woman to one would could meet the challenge of flying comfortably to Spain.

Having said that, I must emphasise that before you do need to put serious time and effort into scheduling and carrying out these rehearsals. Don't allow the fact that they don't take up much time to seduce you thinking they are not important. You may not be an actor, but with time and effort, you will be pleasantly surprised by how well the human mind can execute these visualisations, and how well they work. After she returned from Spain, I asked Suzanne how she thought the transformation happened. She shrugged and said, 'It just happened.' So it will be with you. Concentrate on the technique, believe in what you are doing and it will work.

The first time you begin the work-out, these enabling habits are exciting and novel. As with a physical workout however, with the passage of time, the novelty wears off and maintaining the routines becomes more difficult. To combat this, it's a good idea to record your experiences as you go, keeping a note of the challenges that you have attempted and how well you did. As well as recording your self-talk, note how you transformed it, and observe too how well the WWW works *in addition* to recording and replaying the good stuff.

Some will question whether it's possible to achieve this much change in only 21 days. Take our faltering public speaker for example. It's important to note that the workout routine will raise your performance to the level of your *current potential*. It will allow you to overcome the inner critic, the one who sets out to sabotage your performance, but it will not give you skills which you do not have. You may need to get additional help to improve your actual public speaking competence. And – as with any habit – you will need to persist to keep the habit active. If you do not keep up the workout, those old unwanted behaviours will inevitably return.

Use it or lose it
Self-doubt is an inevitable fact of life. As you try to make these changes, it will rear up and attempt to undermine your efforts. The solution is to dismiss the negative thought, to say to yourself, 'Yes, it's good to be able to look at all sides, but I believe I can do this.'

Too much doubt, if you allow it, can act as a growth retardant. You will need to rely on the conscious mind, on old-fashioned will-power to snap out of it.

What is the single greatest reason for failure? It's the same reason New Year's resolutions fail. People forget, get careless, lapse back into comfort zones, lose enthusiasm and so on. To make this work, you do not have to be an exceptional athlete or scholar or genius, you simply have to be capable of committing to enacting these workouts every single day. Just as a physical workout needs to be maintained to hold onto fitness levels, you need to keep up your mental workout to avoid sliding back into old patterns of behaviour.

To restate, there is nothing mystical or miraculous in this process. You are simply harnessing the natural genius of the human mind to bring about real and lasting change.

7
Worked Examples

An Interview

Challenge: Interview in three weeks for a managerial position with a large, successful IT firm.
Question: What would it be like if I perform at my best?
Trigger Sentence: I am thrilled that I am relaxed and sharp during the interview.

Now use this trigger sentence to pre-enact the interview eight times a day for twenty days before the interview. Remember, the trigger sentence must be personal, it must be present tense and it must always turn out well. Use all the senses to experience the action. Add in background details and atmosphere. Feel the emotion; this is why a word like 'thrilled' is so important in generating the right emotional state.

Now you shoehorn the practice of each simulation into your day, repeating at least eight times. Remember too that you don't have to carry these thoughts in your head as you enter the interview venue. Your subconscious mind has been prepped. Focus only on the process in hand.

A Speech

Challenge: A wedding speech in three weeks' time.
Question: What would it be like if I perform at my best?
Trigger Sentence: I am thrilled that I am relaxed, entertaining and funny as I make my speech.

Plan a walk along a familiar, quiet route twenty days out from the wedding; using the features you meet along the way to trigger your visualisation. Depending on the length of the walk, you can plan between 5 and 10 reps. Find a trigger to begin – a tree, a gateway, whatever. I see myself walking to the stage and lifting the mike, I feel it in my hand, I ask 'Can everyone at the back hear me clearly?' I hear myself saying this and see the heads nodding. Now I wait until I come to another trigger point on the walk, and the second pre-enactment begins. I feel the confidence associated with making a good speech, I see people laughing. I pick out one of the people whom I know will be there and I imagine her laughing along.

Now, I relax and enjoy my walk until the next trigger point calls me back to the task. In this way, you parcel out different parts of the intended speech which you act out in your mind. Remember to conjure up the emotion involved. Feel what it feels like to deliver a speech with confidence and ease. In the next rep, I enjoy the sensations of being on stage, standing up straight and pacing my phrases so all will hear, and I see and hear and feel the emotion of the laughter at a joke I have reserved for this day.

I want to emphasise that these intermittent reps of bits of the speech do not have to be coherent or highly planned to be effective. Our imaginations don't need a command performance to take all of this visualisation on board, to supplant trepidation with excitement and confidence.

A Phobia

Challenge: Overcoming a phobia of birds.

Question: What would it be like if I was no longer terrified of birds?

Trigger Sentence: I am thrilled that I can now tolerate the presence of birds.

This is actually a genuine problem experienced by one of my clients. She had become extremely fearful in the presence of birds, to the point where normal everyday activities like going for a walk along the beach or walking down a city street had become permeated by fear and anxiety. This woman's self-talk – *I've got a thing about birds* – only served to embed this fear and make life more difficult than it was.

As I have pointed out in earlier chapters, the pre-frontal cortex in our brain contains an ingenious device which allows us not only to anticipate future events but also to imagine these events happening in the here and now. We can use this wonderful facility to rehearse any situation through visualisation. Of course, 'visualisation' is something of a misnomer. As you recreate a world free of the fear of birds, you call on the power of all of your senses:

- See yourself doing the action.
- Hear the sounds involved.
- Feel the physical sensations.
- Smell any smells involved.
- Taste anything that might be relevant.

As you recreate an experience, be sure to engage positive emotion. Recite the trigger sentence: *I am thrilled that I can now tolerate the presence of birds.* Now, like a good actor, call on all your senses to conjure up the required experience, this time displacing the anxiety with calm. Like a scene from a film or a play, fill your imaginative visualisation with scenery and background; make it as real as possible. Don't worry if your recreation feels flawed or unreal. With practise, your innate skill at this exercise will take over and you will find your anxiety giving way to composure and serenity.

Remember, the student that is under instruction here is your self-image; that part of you that will put this new habit to good use.

Give one minute to this exercise each time you repeat, slotting these little exercises into spare minutes throughout your day. At the same time, take care to notice and curtail any negative self-talk that seeks to subvert your drive to change your behaviour.

Aim for ten repetitions per day for fourteen days. That gives us a sum total of 140 minutes of pre-experience to drive out the old behaviours and ring in the new. No growth retardant allowed. Nurture the new shoots.

Go.

8
Workout Summary

Remember, your perception of reality is no more than a perception; many of us are naturally predisposed to overstate our weaknesses and understate our strengths. This tendency can lead to a vicious cycle of poor perception – poor performance – poor perception. To break that cycle, it is necessary to address that critical voice.

1. Over a two-week period, carefully document your negative self-talk. Submit each negative perception to the truth test. Are you really failing as badly as you think you are?
2. Positive psychology has thought us other ways of dealing with negative self-talk. The What Went Well exercise, in which positive events are recalled and re-lived has been proven to have a significant positive impact on wellbeing.
3. When facing a challenge, imaginative visualisation is an excellent means of addressing anxiety and greatly increasing the chances of positive performance. Create a trigger sentence which cloaks positive intention with positive emotion. This becomes the launch-pad for a series of imaginative visualisations which prepare you for the challenge ahead.

Three months from when you begin, give yourself a thorough check-up, a mental MOT. Has your self-talk changed? By now it should be transformed. By now, you should experience satisfaction and contentment as well as growing self esteem and confidence.

ACKNOWLEDGEMENTS

My English teacher at Abbey Grammar School in Newry was Brother Pierce McFarland. He was also my Gaelic Football coach, and one of the first men that ever inspired any kind of self-confidence in me. Gerry Brown – the man who would manage the All-Ireland winning Down team of 1968 – was also an inspirational teacher and coach at that school. He would later go on to become a good friend. I also acknowledge Lou Tice as the inspiration behind my interest in the more practical aspects of psychology. I still appreciate the gift of The Winners Circle email, which I read every working day. I also want to acknowledge the great support and inspiration of my family.

Printed in Poland
by Amazon Fulfillment
Poland Sp. z o.o., Wrocław

53466462R00040